Aug 24, 2012

Dear Ma.

MW00975835

Blessings to my
dear brother.
Have a full life ahead
of you lead by the Spirit!

Otto

Seeking God

Dedicated to my brother Rob
Nov. 1, 1955 - July 29, 2009

a Giant of a Man,
Full of Life and Adventure

Otto Schultinge
June, 2009

"God Says So"

Come and visit us at my Facebook® group "God Says So" and post your questions and/or participate in the discussion about matters of God.

To grow in your understanding of who God is, to make sense of this life through a Christian worldview, and to explore a love relationship with Christ.

To get to know God personally, and more importantly to deepen your intimate, love relationship with God the Father, God the Son and God the Holy Spirit.

Scripture quotations are from The Holy Bible, New Living Translation, copyright © 1996, 2004, 2007. Used by permission of Tyndale House Publishers Inc, Carol Stream, Illinois 60188. All right reserved.

ISBN-13: 978-1477518373

Dedication

Rob was loved by so many. He was my older, taller, stronger brother and had a great thirst for life and adventure. He opened my eyes to life's possibilities and showed me how to never give up, but stand tall and go all-out.

As a very capable, well-experienced, and deeply-respected man, he enjoyed life, sailing the seas and oceans, and traveling the world. He also worked hard, and had many friends. He and his wife loved each other deeply and shared beautiful plans together. Life was good.

Then, while in the midst of his full, exciting life, a terrible illness took him away from us. Before his illness, only one thing was lacking in Rob's life: an unconditional love, giving him deep joy, lasting peace, and solid hope. This kind of love comes only from God.

I wrote this book to help my brother find real peace, to give him hope amidst all the misery, and to share in the joy I had found through the love of God. May it help to introduce you to the godly love we all so desperately need.

With love, Otto

A Personal Note

This is a personal journey asking many questions in an effort to find life's answers. It is not meant to be read in one sitting, but rather over a forty-day period. The intention is to stimulate daily thinking about the ideas presented.

Each daily reading will loosely build on the previous day. I encourage you to form an opinion about the ideas, the logic and the "train of thought" presented each day, prior to reading the next day's material. It is not necessary to agree with everything presented. It is all about the big picture.

This is a most exciting journey. If this book does nothing else, it will address three very important questions: "Where did I come from?", "Who is God?", and "Where will I find love?"

While you take this journey, meditation will help give you inspiration or, if you are comfortable doing so, you may want to pray for God's guidance and answers. May this journey help discover amazing truths as it unfolds life's mysteries and leads you to eternal joy.

Introduction

If someone asked you what was the most crucial moment or experience in your life, how would you answer? Has anything in your life caused you to shift gears and dramatically change your life's direction? What comes to mind? An accident? The loss of a loved one? Divorce, financial ruin, or sickness? Has a life-long, cherished dream been shattered?

But what about a positive life-defining moment? Has something ever happened to you that drastically affected your life in an all-out positive way? If so, you may have experienced a paradigm shift, causing you to see the world as a entirely different place. And you are totally awestruck! That is what this story is about—an encounter with the one living, true God.

There is a God unlike anything we normally hear about in our history and philosophy classes. He is different from anything we read about in popular magazines or novels and he is not the God portrayed in most movies. Rather, the God we will meet will be understood and experienced at a personal level. This Heavenly Father, who embodies love and power, truth and glory, eagerly waits to welcome all his children home.

Creator

Day One: Before the Beginning

It is dark–very, very dark.
It is silent, the universe empty.

There is no light, no sound, no stars, no planets.
There is nothing–no space, no time, no universe.

Can we imagine this? What did the universe look like before it existed? Wait a minute! Can anything look like something before it exists? Impossible, right?

Science is now quite clear about a point in time in which the universe came into existence. With the eruption of the universe came space and time. Actually, the universe came into existence at the very moment time and space emerged, out of nothing, from nothing.

How difficult to grasp and how beautiful to discover this truth. What caused this massive occurrence to happen? How could all there is, emerge from nothing? Can anything come from nothing? If there once was nothing, why now do we have something? Logic says 'out of nothing can come nothing.' Therefore, something must have always existed.

* Suggested further reading: God Are You There? - William Lane Craig

Genesis 1:1-5

In the beginning God created the heavens and the earth. The earth was formless and empty, and darkness covered the deep waters. And the Spirit of God was hovering over the surface of the waters. Then God said, "Let there be light", and there was light. And God saw that the light was good. Then he separated the light from the darkness. God called the light "day" and the darkness "night".

Note:
The very first words in the Bible claim God created the universe and all life in it. Do we believe the word of God and recognize His creation?

Day Two: The Uncaused Cause

Everything is caused by something. Makes sense, right? If something causes another something to happen, we can imagine an enormous chain reaction of events unfolding. Each event causes a reaction, right to the present time. Now let us go backwards and discover the original cause that set this chain reaction into motion. Here are two options:

First, the chain reaction is endless. In other words, there is no beginning. As long as we go back in time, there will always be yet another cause. We'll never get to the point of the original cause that sets everything in motion. An honest man will recognize the foolishness of this. By allowing the chain reaction to go back into infinity, we avoid the most simple question of origins: "Why is there something, rather than nothing?" Or in other words: "What caused the very first event?" Rather than avoiding those questions, shouldn't we embrace them? Those questions, after all, help us define the meaning of life.

Second, the chain reaction is not endless. Therefore, it has a beginning. It has an original cause, which itself is uncaused. This is referred to as the Uncaused Cause. From this Uncaused Cause, everything that exists originates. By some, this is also known as God.

* Suggested further reading: Does the Idea of God make Sense? - Charles Taliaferro

Revelation 1:8

"I am the Alpha and the Omega–the beginning and the end," says the Lord God. "I am the one who is, who always was, and who is still to come–the Almighty One."

Note:
The Bible is quite clear about God being the uncaused cause. As the Alpha and Omega, the beginning and the end, God is the cause of all.

Day Three: Alive or Dead?

So here we are. We stand before the beginning of time, before the existence of the universe, before anything at all. All that exists is the Uncaused Cause, which always was, always is and always will be, the very origin of all that is, and the reason for existence.

What can we know about the Uncaused Cause (God), if anything? Allow me a free and short interpretation.

> "One Monday morning,
> sometime after breakfast,
> God made a decision
> and pushed *a button*,
> the Big Bang button.
> *BBAAAANNNNGG!*
> echoed through the void....
> And the rest, as they say, is history."

Okay, it probably did not happen this way. There was no button to push and no breakfast to eat. But what we can confidently say is this: God, the Uncaused Cause, set the chain reaction in motion. For whatever reason, God started it all. A decision was made. He caused the universe into existence.

This is huge. Dead nothingness doesn't make decisions or cause explosions. Dead gods don't push buttons. Our God is alive!

Hebrews 4:12-13

For the word of God is alive and powerful. It is sharper than the sharpest two-edged sword, cutting between soul and spirit, between joint and marrow. It exposes our innermost thoughts and desires. Nothing in all creation is hidden from God. Everything is naked and exposed before his eyes, and he is the one to whom we are accountable.

Note:
For God to be able to create, He must be alive, but the Bible claims even more. Not only is God alive, His Word (the Bible) is as well. When we seek God and read His Word, He comes alive through it, to us.

Day Four: Awake or Asleep?

It has been said, "God is dead." He may be dead in people's minds, but the truth is that He is very much alive in the Universe. God is the Uncaused Cause, the origin of all that exists and everything that is. Without God nothing exists. He exists, therefore we exist.

God existed before time. He is beyond time. He transcends time. He does not get older or younger. He does not change. He cannot change. Change happens over time. It is impossible for God.

So perhaps He is asleep. You know, He grew tired after creating the Universe over the course of those six very long days and, then, on the seventh day He rested and fell asleep. Can spirits fall asleep? Can we even imagine a god causing the Universe to come into existence and then becoming bored with it and falling asleep?

We must grasp is the universe's total dependence on God. All energy, all natural laws, all stars, all life, everything that has been created came from the mind of God and was then spoken into existence. Without God, His creation would simply cease to exist. As long as we live and move and have our being, we can be sure that God is awake and alert.

* Suggested further reading: Defending Your Faith - RC Sproul

Isaiah 40:28-31

Have you never heard? Have you never understood? The Lord
is the everlasting God, the Creator of all the earth. He never
grows weak or weary. No one can measure the depths of his
understanding. He gives power to the weak and strength to the
powerless. Even youths will become weak and tired, and young
men will fall in exhaustion. But those who trust in the Lord will
find new strength. They will soar high
on wings like eagles. They will run and not grow weary. They
will walk and not faint.

Note:
For those of us who know God, He is more than alive. Isaiah's
words, as inspired by God, speak the truth. An intimate
relationship with the everlasting God will let us soar like eagles.

Day Five: Personal Perhaps?

We humans act and interact with outside forces. It is what life is all about, a constant acting and reacting to our surroundings. Each of us observe, analyze, decide and behave in our own unique way. One person may laugh, while another may cry. We have our own personalities and wills, which determine the course of our actions. Our inner person (the mind, will, and emotions) makes a choice, causing behavior that echoes that choice.

What about an impersonal force? Can an impersonal force make a decision? Can gravity, for instance, ever do anything consciously? How about electricity? It can kill you or light up your day, but does it do so knowingly?

What about Energy or Love? Are they alive or dead? Can they make decisions or push buttons? It's silly even to think so, isn't it? To make a decision, they would not only have to be alive, they would have to be sentient.. Dead matter cannot do anything, but impersonal forces cannot do much either, other than obey the laws of nature.

Here is the sum of the matter: God decided to act and create. An impersonal God wouldn't be able to act or create; Only a personal God can. Therefore, as evidenced by a dynamic creation, God is a personal being, alive and alert.

Deuteronomy 31:6

So be strong and courageous! Do not be afraid and do not panic before them. For the Lord your God will personally go ahead of you. He will neither fail you nor abandon you.

Note:
What a difference this makes. A personal God interested in participating in our lives–guiding us, protecting us, loving us. It seems too good to be true, but is it?

Day Six: Creator & Creation

God created the universe. Out of nothing, God spoke and the cosmos exploded into existence. The magnitude of that explosion, the power at play, and the energy displayed are unimaginable. The universe started its expansion at immeasurable speeds and continues to grow even today. Stars were born, 200 to 300 billion galaxies were formed and amidst all this seeming chaos, God established order.

Then God created Adam and Eve in the Garden of Eden, marking the start of mankind's history. Mankind dwells in perfect harmony with all of creation and especially with God our Father. Among the stars, planets and everything else created on our beautiful earth, we were created unique and special. Actually, we humans are the crown of His creation. We are created in His image. We are the reflection of His very being.

As the Uncaused Cause, alive and personal, God decided His existence would be enriched by His creation. He knew full well the struggles we would face. Because He transcends time, nothing surprises Him, which means He knew the end of the story before it even began. When He agreed to create life and call it into existence, He wasn't afraid to risk our happiness. God, saw that the end of the story would be full of glory—a glory we may share forever with Him. But, I get ahead of myself. So far, all I have established is that God is alive and personal. Could an Uncaused Cause be anything else?

Genesis 1:26-28

Then God said, "Let us make human beings in our image, to be like ourselves. They will reign over the fish in the sea, the birds in the sky, the livestock, all the wild animals on the earth, and the small animals that scurry along the ground." So God created human beings in his own image. In the image of God he created them; male and female he created them. Then God blessed them and said, "Be fruitful and multiply. Fill the earth and govern it. Reign over the fish in the sea, the birds in the sky, and all the animals that scurry along the ground.

Note:
It gets better and better, doesn't it? From an unknown idea or some kind of impersonal force, we get introduced to the idea that God is a living, personal being interested and involved in His creation. On top of that, He wants us to know He created us in His image. Ever wonder why?

Creation

Day Seven: Mother Earth

Our little planet seems insignificant among the vast cosmos, but science proves otherwise. On this planet, earth, conditions are perfect to sustain life. If just one of these hundreds of specific conditions were any different, life on earth would cease to exist.

Consider: Other heavenly bodies contribute to our vitality. Our unusually large moon is a stabilizing anchor, protecting us, causing tides, and lighting up the night. Jupiter functions as our cosmos vacuum due to its extreme gravity. Our perfect sun is exactly the right age, size, temperature and distance from us.

Our earth is just the right size to hold our atmosphere. It has the perfect strength magnetic field, and it has a core of the exact required thickness. Our earth holds an abundance of water, essential for life processes and the correct amount required for a stable climate. Furthermore, our water reflects, stores and releases all the energy needed for life.

These are just a few of the "just right" conditions of the earth and its position in our solar system. No wonder people address her as Mother Earth. But we shouldn't be thankful to her. It is God our Father who needs to be thanked. We shall soon discover how God, the Intelligent Designer, planned it all for our sake.

*Suggested further reading: The Case for a Creator - Lee Strobel

Matthew 6:9-13

Pray like this: Our Father in heaven, may your name be kept holy. May your Kingdom come soon. May your will be done on earth, as it is in heaven. Give us today the food we need, and forgive us our sins, as we have forgiven those who sin against us. And don't let us yield to temptation, but rescue us from the evil one.

Note:
The God of the bible is in fact our heavenly Father. With Him we experience unconditional love, wherever we are on our journey. He looks out for us, holds our hands, guides us through life and even carries us when times get tough.

Day Eight: Chance Theory

Take a die and throw a six. What is the chance of that happening? Your chance is one in six. Not a good chance, but it's possible. How about throwing a six 200 times in a row? That is practically impossible, wouldn't you think? Common sense says there is a zero percent chance. It has a chance of 0.1^{156} .

There are approximately 200 critical conditions to make the earth life-friendly. Some are highly critical with almost zero variance allowed in order to achieve life-friendly conditions. Others are less critical but essential nonetheless. Could that happen by chance? It is the equivalent of throwing a six with your die—200 times in a row.

Some argue there are as many as 300 billion galaxies (11 zeroes) with billions of stars and planets each (another 11 zeroes). "Surely some of those planets will have similar conditions to Earth. How can our planet be one of a kind?" The odds of this happening by chance are just as preposterous. When we multiply a chance of 0.1^{156} (rolling a six, 200 times in a row) with 10^{22} (the number of galaxies and planets), the result is 0.1^{134}, nil chance and I rest my case.

* Suggested further reading: Fatal Flaws - Hank Hanegraaff

Colossians 1:15-16

Christ is the visible image of the invisible God. He existed before anything was created and is supreme over all creation, for through him God created everything in the heavenly realms and on earth.

Note:
We have two extreme alternatives. One is a cold and impersonal universe that lacks passion and purpose. The other is a personal God Who created us, loves us dearly, and does everything possible to enter our lives.

Day Nine: Intelligent Designer

Millennia ago, earth's scholars discovered order in this world. "Look," they said, "every twenty-four-hour cycle, the sun rises and sets during the day, and each night the moon accompanies us. Every twenty-nine days the moon waxes and wanes—a complete cycle from new to full. Every 365 days we experience the same four seasons. . . ."

Over the centuries, scholars have recognized this order in our vast universe, such as planets orbiting in precise, timely fashion around stars. In recent decades, scholars have also discovered intricate design on a molecular level. We can confidently claim all of creation is defined by order and design.

Where do order and design come from? Are they natural, by-chance phenomena or rather clear signs of intelligence? We can accept a universe organizing itself naturally by chance, with order and design emerging as yet another lucky streak. Or we can choose the alternative and acknowledge the presence of an intelligent designer.

When we open our eyes and recognize a designed universe rather than a chaotic one, it will not be hard to conclude there is a designer. It certainly seems we need less faith to believe in an Intelligent Designer than in mere chaos. What do you say?

* Suggested further reading: The Design Revolution - William A. Dembski

Proverbs 1:1-7

These are the proverbs of Solomon, David's son, king of Israel. Their purpose is to teach people wisdom and discipline, to help them understand the insights of the wise. Their purpose is to teach people to live disciplined and successful lives, to help them do what is right, just, and fair. These proverbs will give insight to the simple, knowledge and discernment to the young. Let the wise listen to these proverbs and become even wiser. Let those with understanding receive guidance by exploring the meaning in these proverbs and parables, the words of the wise and their riddles. Fear of the Lord is the foundation of true knowledge, but fools despise wisdom and discipline.

Note:
It is a frightening thought to accept God is real and personal, and on top of that, 'all-knowing.' It's a good thing He loves us no matter what.

Day Ten: Slime & Time

Life is extraordinary. The enormous difference between "alive" and "dead" is hard to ignore and yet many think life can somehow emerge from dead matter. Some say that, over time and given the right conditions, life can begin by its own forces, out of the primordial soup. With lots of slime and time, life will miraculously emerge.

There are some real problems with this. (1) Chance theory shows the virtual impossibility of all necessary ingredients for life to come together at just the right time, at just the right place, in the right quantities, in the right sequence, in the right manner, etc. (2) Combining a number of dead components does not result in life. Dead is dead. (3) Random forces work against order and instead result in chaos. Life, on the other hand, consists of an extremely well-organized, very finely tuned process.

And then there is the question of what came first, the chicken or the egg? Life can reproduce itself through information found within its DNA. Without DNA, there is no life. But for DNA to exist, we need a cell to manufacture it. DNA can't exist outside a cell. So, how can we explain the sudden existence of both DNA and living cells? This is a dilemma we can't overcome without the assistance of a creator.

* Suggested further reading: Unshakable Foundations - Norman Geisler & Peter Bocchino

Psalms 77:13-14

O God, your ways are holy.
Is there any god as mighty as you?
You are the God of great wonders!

Note:

Isn't it crazy, all the hoops we jump through, just to have an excuse not to believe in God? In reality, life is simple.

Accepting God and receiving His love is nothing less than the greatest miracle we will ever experience.

Day Eleven: DNA I Say

With the discovery of DNA, the world looked different. A world with obvious order and design receives even greater structure and detail when we learn about and understand elegant DNA strands, that are full of remarkable information. We now know DNA is the code of life, the key to cell form and function.

DNA (deoxyribonucleic acid) is a code, similar to a computer's script of zeros and ones. By combining the four letters in different combinations, DNA holds the instruction for cell reproduction, actually the genetic instructions used in the development and functioning of all known living organisms. The amount of data DNA can handle is comparable to the entire Encyclopedia Britannica, with over 20 million words covering the breadth of human knowledge.

There is simply no way to collect this amount of information without intelligent guidance. Believing that a living cell could emerge by chance is the same as believing that a group of monkeys could miraculously type a "Harry Potter" novel.

With DNA we are, yet again, faced with the possibility of a higher, creative power. DNA provides more evidence, so necessary for that paradigm shift all earnest seekers of truth will eventually experience. The existence of a living, intelligent, creative, uncaused Designer starts to make sense. A lot of it!

* Suggested further reading: Creation as Science - Hugh Ross

Romans 1:25

They traded the truth about God for a lie. So they worshiped and served the things God created instead of the Creator himself, who is worthy of eternal praise! Amen.

Note:
What kind of lie can hide the truth that is behind the DNA, embedded in each cell of all living beings? Do we consciously keep the blindfold in place as we are too scared to face God? Don't we get it? His grace is endless!

Day Twelve: Mouse Trap

Heard of the "mousetrap principle" or irreducible complexity? This describes a device or system in which all components work together so intricately the device would no longer function if even one component was missing. Take a mousetrap, for instance, and determine how its components function together in a specific manner. Without the platform, spring, hammer or catch, it would be useless. It would cease to function.

Living organisms are full of these complex systems. A good example is the bacterial flagellum. some say it is the most efficient motor in the universe. It consists of 30 to 35 components and, in principal, is similar to an outboard motor on a boat. Without a propeller or shaft, an outboard rotary motor does not function.

Likewise, the flagellum motor works only after it is mature and complete. But during its gradual development over thousands of generations, it would have to have the same "irreducible complexity," or it would fail to function. How can this be reconciled with evolution's core principle of small and slow improvements in the organism's ability to survive? Carrying around an incomplete motor, generation after generation, would not increase the organism's ability to survive, but rather incomplete components would create such a burden that the organism would cease to exist.

* Suggested further reading: The Case for a Creator - Lee Strobel

Psalms 111:1-4

Praise the Lord!

I will thank the Lord with all my heart as I meet with his godly people.

How amazing are the deeds of the Lord!

All who delight in him should ponder them.

Everything he does reveals his glory and majesty.

His righteousness never fails.

He causes us to remember his wonderful works.

How gracious and merciful is our Lord!

Note:

It's awesome and amazing to recognize God's hand in creation. Why do we try so hard to keep God out of it? Life is truly more beautiful with God in it.

Day Thirteen: Macro or Micro?

Micro-evolution is real. Evolution within the species occurs to help them adjust to their environment. Examples include a giraffe growing a longer neck to better survive and a moth developing camouflage to blend in with its surroundings. These occur beyond a doubt. Macro-evolution, on the other hand, is problomatic. This type of very slow, small-step-by-small-step, generation-after-generation evolution from one species into another does not occur.

Darwin presented his theory not as proven, but as pending following confirmation by the discovery of fossils of "incomplete," "half/half," "in-between stage" specimens. Many of these fossils would be found, he argued, due to the very long period over which these evolutions take place. If they were never discovered, he would consider his theory null and void.

A problem remains: The missing links are still missing. Even if the handful of fossils presented as proof weren't fraudulent, Darwin would still not have considered his theory proven. Real proof would mean the discovery of thousands upon thousands of fossils that could not be labeled as belonging to any of the known species, but rather as "in-between stages" creatures. After 150 years and the discovery of millions of fossils of genuine species, the case to confirm his theory is now closed. His theory has proven false.

* Suggested further reading: The Farce of Evolution - Hank Hanegraaff

Matthew 6:19-21

Don't store up treasures here on earth, where moths eat them and rust destroys them, and where thieves break in and steal. Store your treasures in heaven, where moths and rust cannot destroy, and thieves do not break in and steal. Wherever your treasure is, there the desires of your heart will also be.

Note:
We can choose to hunt for missing links and in the process delay the inevitable. Or we can focus on God and be introduced to life's real treasures.

Day Fourteen: Against All Odds

Naturalism's challenge has four theorems. First, nature must create itself out of absolute nothingness. Second, nature must go against itself and create order out of chaos and design out of randomness. Third, nature must create life out of inert dead matter, and this by chance. Finally, nature must do all this without intelligence, creativity, decisiveness, vision, or being alive. What a tall order to achieve all four objectives!

Let's see how logic fails these presuppositions. First, can something really come out of nothing? When there is absolute nothingness, there are simply no building blocks to create anything. Out of nothing, no thing can come. Second, how can order and design come out of chaos and randomness? Chaos by itself can never result in order. Design requires intelligence, while randomness does not require it. What unintelligent, random forces can arrange chaos into order? Third, can inert, dead matter turn into life? Time doesn't matter, so very slow, small-step-by-small-step, generation-after-generation changes will not occur. Dead is stone dead, and will remain dead.

Believing in nature's ability to do all of the above requires a stunning amount of faith. If we stand on solid ground and objectively view the world in which we live, believing in an Uncaused Cause, Creator, or Intelligent Designer is a much more reasonable alternative. Naturalism seems against all odds.

* Suggested further reading: The universe next door - James W. Sire

Isaiah 45:18-19

For the Lord is God, and he created the heavens and earth
and put everything in place.
He made the world to be lived in, not to be a place of empty
chaos.
"I am the Lord," he says, "and there is no other.
I publicly proclaim bold promises.
I do not whisper obscurities in some dark corner.
I would not have told the people of Israel to seek me if I could
not be found.
I, the Lord, speak only what is true and declare only what is
right."

Note:
Once we come to grips with the futility of denying God's
creation, a new, exciting and lifelong journey will start. That is
coming to know our creator God.

God

Day Fifteen: O, O, O

From now on, we will refer to the Uncaused Cause, Creator, and Intelligent Designer as God. We've reasoned that any force responsible for the creation of the universe, for a life-friendly environment, and for life itself cannot be impersonal, or dead energy. Rather, this force is a creative, personal, living God. What else can we know about this God?

God is outside the time and space continuum and therefore is not limited by it. God is "bigger than the universe He created," which means in practicality that God is present anywhere and everywhere at all times. He is omnipresent.

God created the universe, therefore all power and all knowledge contained within it derive from Him. Nothing created can be more powerful or more knowledgeable than its creator. God knows it all, and He can do it all. He is omniscient and omnipotent.

Imagining the infinite power, intelligence, and presence of God is impossible. We cannot get even a glimpse of the true essence of God. Getting to know Him, though, is part of the journey He has invited us to participate in. Becoming more familiar with His character is an exercise in discovering purity and love, unlike anything we have ever or will ever experience.

* Suggested further reading: The Character of God - RC Sproul

Job 28:23-28

"God alone understands the way to wisdom; he knows where it can be found, for he looks throughout the whole earth and sees everything under the heavens. He decided how hard the winds should blow and how much rain should fall. He made the laws for the rain and laid out a path for the lightning. Then he saw wisdom and evaluated it. He set it in place and examined it thoroughly. And this is what he says to all humanity: 'The fear of the Lord is true wisdom; to forsake evil is real understanding.'"

Note:
With our finite brains, we will never fully grasp the infinite wisdom of God. It may not be such a bad idea for us to pay attention to His word, especially since He loves to guide us toward heaven.

Day Sixteen: Holy, Holy, Holy

Perhaps we were once privileged to meet a famous artist, or powerful ruler, or wealthy king. The more we look up to that person, the more nervous we would be. Imagine now meeting the God who is responsible for the creation of the universe and all of life in it.

Impossible, right? We cannot even think how majestic God truly is. How could we ever imagine meeting Him? Yet, the ultimate experience for any of us would be to come face to face with God. To be in the presence of Almighty God and see Him would truly be the most profound experience of our lives. Unfortunately, we would not live to tell of it. The pure brightness of God is more blinding than the sun; His supremacy is greater than all the forces of the universe combined. We would die before ever laying eyes on Him. Blinded by His overpowering brightness and in awe of His infinite grandness, we would instantly cease to exist.

God is vastly different from anything we have ever known or imagined. He is set apart. God transcends everything and anything we know. He holds all the superlatives ever known to man and any superlatives with which we are unfamiliar. He is the Alpha and Omega, the beginning and the end. He is holy, holy, holy—altogether right and correct in all He is.

* Suggested further reading: The Holiness of God - RC Sproul

Revelation 4:8

Holy, holy, holy
is the Lord God, the Almighty—
the one who always was,
who is, and who is still to come.

Note:
The holiness of God humbles us. What can we say or do in
the presence of a holy God? As we will see, it is a good thing
unconditional love is part of being holy.

Day Seventeen: God's Love

Is God a good God? With all the pain and suffering in the world, is it still possible that He is a good God? Some argue and say, "God is either incapable of running His affairs on earth, or He is not good. If God were good and capable, He would never allow all this evil." Is there another explanation that captures God role in our lives and the universe at large?

We must recognize the world we live in is no longer the paradise He created. It is a fallen world just as we also are fallen creatures. He has given us free choice and He respects the choices we make. Mind you He is right there with us, holding our hands as we deal with the consequences of those choices. He warns us of course and guides us through thick and thin. But it's up to us to follow through.

God could speak the word and all would be perfect. But He also values real, intimate love relationships, respectful of who we are and what we choose to do. He cares for all of mankind and is actively involved in keeping this universe running.

God doesn't cause the mess in life. It's us! We cause the pain. And without taking away our freedom and free will, He remains control of the universe and unfolds His master plan. Our Heavenly Father continues to love us unconditionally.

* Suggested further reading: What's So Amazing about Grace? - Philip Yancey

1 Corinthians 13: 4-7

Love is patient and kind. Love is not jealous or boastful or proud or rude. It does not demand its own way. It is not irritable, and it keeps no record of being wronged. It does not rejoice about injustice but rejoices whenever the truth wins out. Love never gives up, never loses faith, is always hopeful, and endures through every circumstance.

Note:
The problem of evil is huge. The good news is that the Bible explains the origin of evil, conquers it through the love of God and is definite about an evil-free world to come. With God there is real hope.

Day Eighteen: God's Glory

God is the only fully independent living being in existence. He is the Uncaused Cause. Nothing existed before Him and all that has ever existed has its origin in Him. Therefore nothing can increase or decrease who He is. He is unchangeable. So what possibly can motivate God? What are God's interests? Does anything move Him?

We know one thing: God is a relational being, just as we are. The quality of our relationships is the key to determining the true fulfillment and enjoyment we experience in life. Even the creation of human life itself, with each newborn baby, is meant to be the result of two beings in loving harmony with each other. The secret to increasing joy in your life is to improve your relationships with each other.

This is what God focuses upon: building personal relationships with each and every one of us. In building these personal relationships, we come to know Him. It is a lifetime process because His infinite character cannot be boxed in. His love, purity and power will forever astound us and, as we learn to relate to Him as our Heavenly Father, our lives will never be the same again. We will worship Him and glorify Him. God's glory will reign.

* Suggested further reading: God as He Longs for You to See Him - Chip Ingram

Jeremiah 13:15-17

Listen and pay attention!
Do not be arrogant, for the Lord has spoken.
Give glory to the Lord your God before it is too late.
Acknowledge him before he brings darkness upon you, causing
you to stumble and fall on the darkening mountains.
For then, when you look for light, you will find only terrible
darkness and gloom.
And if you still refuse to listen, I will weep alone because of
your pride.
My eyes will overflow with tears, because the Lord's flock will
be led away into exile.

Note:
The contrast between glory and doom is incomprehensible.
According to the Bible heaven and hell are real. We will share
in God's glory or be doomed to darkness. That is *our* choice.

Day Nineteen: Paradise Lost

After God completed the Garden of Eden, man's paradise on earth, He breathed life into Adam and Eve, the first humans to walk the earth. God saw them as His most wonderful creation. They reflected His image and were given what no other being on earth enjoyed: a conscience. Adam and Eve were aware of who they were, creations of God. They walked the garden, recognizing and enjoying its beauty. They loved each other and found themselves literally in paradise. They enjoyed freedom of choice and knew no sin. Most important, they were in awe of God. They loved Him and worshiped Him as their Heavenly Father.

God was pleased. He loved them very much and they loved Him back. He entrusted the garden into their care, His plan from the beginning and for all eternity. Their job was to multiply and subdue the earth, to cultivate the Garden of Eden, name the animals, and more. They were to live in perfect harmony with all of God's creation and to enjoy a deep loving relationship with Him as their Heavenly Father.

All was good until Satan showed up. He knew we were granted freedom of choice, also about the pure love from God we enjoy. Satan set into motion the inevitable. He lied to Adam and Eve and they, in turn, acted against God's will. Together, they brought sin into the world. Adam and Eve's perfect relationship with God was broken. Paradise was lost.

Job 9:2-4

Yes, I know all this is true in principle.
But how can a person be declared
Innocent in God's sight?
If someone wanted to take God to court,
would it be possible to answer him
even once in a thousand times?
For God is so wise and so mighty.
Who has ever challenged him successfully?

Note:
In the beginning, it was all perfect and, then, it was perfect no
more. Shall we question God about His intentions or inability to
keep paradise intact? Or do we agree with Job?

Man

Day Twenty: Imperfection

When imperfect people are given freedom of choice, sooner or later they make a bad decision. In Adam and Eve's case, it went deadly wrong. God warned them not to eat from the Tree of Knowledge of Good and Evil. He told them they would surely die if they ate the tree's fruit. It was a simple rule to follow.

The fruit of that tree was not more special than the fruit of the other trees. It simply was a means to demonstrate God's law. It would come to reveal their eventual disobedience. By disobeying and eating from the tree, they committed mankind's first sin against God. Thus, they were introduced to the concept of evil. The fruit had no power to open their eyes. It was their own act of disobedience that taught them evil. In the process of eating, they were blinded from His truth and love.

Imperfection causes serious problems. But did God create us as imperfect beings? The truth is, God designed us with freewill. He wanted, and still wants humans who will choose to love Him without being forced to do so. Freedom of choice, even for us imperfect beings, is essential for God's creation. Although we are imperfect, we are also created in His perfect image. We hold the promise of perfection.

Romans 3:19-23

Obviously, the law applies to those to whom it was given, for its purpose is to keep people from having excuses, and to show that the entire world is guilty before God. For no one can ever be made right with God by doing what the law commands. The law simply shows us how sinful we are. But now God has shown us a way to be made right with him without keeping the requirements of the law, as was promised in the writings of Moses and the prophets long ago. We are made right with God by placing our faith in Jesus Christ. And this is true for everyone who believes, no matter who we are. For everyone has sinned; we all fall short of God's glorious standard.

Note:
None of us are any better than Adam and Eve. We are simply all guilty. But in His infinite wisdom, God made a way to save His creation from doom while maintaining His integrity and perfect, sinless being.

Day Twenty-one: Deadly Freedom

God's plan for mankind is for us to love Him. We were perfectly created as relational beings for the purpose of love. Love requires freewill and freedom of choice, which we were given, even if this gift resulted in deadly consequences.

Unlike animals, we are not programmed with certain instinctive characteristics. God could have given us an instinct to adore Him continually, without free choice. Then our love for God would not have mattered one bit. God faced an enormous challenge. Could He create a being with freewill, having the choice to love Him or not, and still guarantee a devoted follower? In other words, given the option that this creature of freewill would reject Him, did He still believe that love would ultimately win?

There are no surprises for God. He knew what would happen in the Garden of Eden. He gave us the ability to disobey and deny Him. God also knew His intimate personal relationship with mankind would be broken. He, in turn, would have to deny access to the Tree of Life forever. The wages of sin would be death.

God realized the steep price mankind paid for their transgressions. He assumed the fee, and was willing to pay a price even more severe. He knew that, in the end, His love would conquer all evil and mankind would be set free from sin for good.

Matthew 22:36-40

"Teacher, which is the most important commandment in the law of Moses?" Jesus replied, "'You must love the Lord your God with all your heart, all your soul, and all your mind.' This is the first and greatest commandment. A second is equally important: 'Love your neighbor as yourself.' The entire law and all the demands of the prophets are based on these two commandments."

Note:
To live a perfect life, all we need to do is follow the above two commandments. The bad news: By ourselves, we are unable. The good news? With God we *are* able.

Day Twenty-two: Mirror Mirror

Most of us probably don't know any murderers. Most people are decent, law-abiding citizens, interested in doing the right thing. Imagine what the world would look like if most of us were criminals. Our societies would be much worse than we now experience. But let's ask an opposite question: "What would tho world look like if all of us perfectly obeyed the Ten Commandments?"

This is where mankind fails to score. Even if we never commit murder, we still fail to obey the sixth commandment: you must not murder. Hating somebody is the same as committing murder in one's mind. Similarly, lust is just like committing adultery in the mind. What about stealing or lying or coveting? The truth is we are all guilty of disobeying every single one of the Ten Commandments.

We may not be all that bad compared to other people. Perhaps we're better than average, but that is not the standard God intends for us. His goodness is the standard. We need to look into the mirror and ask ourselves what we would be like if we were more like God intended us to be. Can we imagine being a saint? Do we even want to be a saint? Though we all fail to achieve God's standard, He does not give up on us. He wants us to take a long look in the mirror. Don't let the mirror lie. Do we see a saint? If we are honest, the answer is no.

Exodus 20:1-17

Then God gave the people all these instructions:
I am the Lord your God, who rescued you from the land of
Egypt, the place of your slavery.
You must not have any other god but me.
You must not make for yourself an idol of any kind.
You must not misuse the name of the Lord your God.
Remember to observe the Sabbath day by keeping it holy.
Honor your father and mother.
You must not murder.
You must not commit adultery.
You must not steal.
You must not testify falsely against your neighbor.
You must not covet.

Note:
Following these Ten Commandments to the letter of the law is
one thing, but God expects us to follow these by the spirit of
the law. Again completely impossible, that is, without God's
help.

Day Twenty-three: Relativity

Take a piece of paper and draw a long straight line, then write the name "Hitler" on one end and "God" on the other end. This line represents the relative goodness of Hitler compared to the absolute goodness of God. Now, pick a place somewhere on the line that represents our own goodness relative to God. Do we place it closer to God, closer to Hitler, or somewhere in the middle?

Most of us will choose incorrectly, because we are ignorant about God's true nature. He is the ultimate in goodness. All love originates from Him. His love and purity are absolute. Even the best among us pale in His presence.

Truthfully, our goodness compared to God's goodness is right next to Hitler's. Just because we recognize Hitler as one of the worst people who ever lived, we can not place him much farther away from God than we. All of us, from the worst to the best, are all sinful people relative to God and His goodness. Of course, since we are able to recognize evil, we should strive to fight it and cultivate goodness. But, no matter how hard we try, we cannot reach God's standard. His is perfection; ours is not.

* Suggested further reading: True for You, but Not for Me - Paul Copan

Job 25:2-6

God is powerful and dreadful.
He enforces peace in the heavens.
Who is able to count
his heavenly army?
Doesn't his light shine on all the earth?
How can a mortal
be innocent before God?
Can anyone born of a woman be pure?
God is more glorious than the moon;
he shines brighter than the stars.
In comparison, people are maggots;
we mortals are mere worms.

Note:
Compared to God, we seem like worms. But once we have
God in our lives, something interesting happens. We are
humbled to the point of full surrender to God, and at the same
time our confidence gets the biggest boost ever. We're now
part of God's family, fully accepted and loved.

Day Twenty-four: Lesson Learned

History repeats itself over and over. Experiences by former generations are forgotten. Mankind is stuck in cycles of war and peace, growth and decline, abundance and poverty.

The Old Testament is a fantastic historical account of a stubborn people. Over and over, the Jewish people would get into trouble, but God would come back, time and time again, to save them. Their trouble was always for the same reason: disobedience!

When they focused on their Lord God Almighty, they prospered and overcame their many great difficulties. Then they became affluent, focused on their own abilities, forgot who was in charge, and things took a turn for the worse. They lost their possessions, their land, even their lives. In the midst of their suffering, they remembered the Lord God Almighty, repented of their sins, and God once again came to their rescue.

There is a lesson to be learned, here. We continue to depend solely on ourselves and we lose track of who God really is. Our sinful nature makes us forget our true origin and distances us from God. Luckily, it is not all lost. We are God's children and He wants us back in His arms.

* Suggested further reading: Can Man Live Without God - Ravi Zacharias

Isaiah 48:17-18

This is what the Lord says—
your Redeemer, the Holy One of Israel:
"I am the Lord your God,
who teaches you what is good for you
and leads you along the paths
you should follow.
Oh, that you had listened
to my commands!
Then you would have had peace
flowing like a gentle river
and righteousness rolling over you
like waves in the sea."

Note:

I'm amazed how patient God is with His people. Even when we do not listen to Him, He keeps on loving us. If only we would trust and love Him unconditionally, we would get a taste of paradise.

Day Twenty-five: Man's Nature

Speaking of learning, which is perceived as more difficult, learning to be good or learning to be bad? What comes more naturally?

As young children, we quickly figure out how to lie, steal, and covet. Kids excel at these "skills", even without parental instruction! Parents struggle to teach their kids to discern right from wrong because it takes continuous effort to explain the difference between good and evil.

In his letter to the Romans, the apostle Paul had something interesting to say about this. He said, "I want to do what is right, but I don't do it. Instead, I do what I hate." He was pointing at the internal struggle we all share, between doing right and wrong. Our nature is inclined to do what is wrong, even though we have a sense of what is right.

We all want to be good and try to do what is right, but we fail constantly. It is as if we are slaves to sin, bound by its destructive power and unable to overcome its grip. We have good intentions but fail nonetheless. If our nature is so inclined to do the wrong thing, how can we ever expect to approach God's standard? What is our way out?

* Suggested further reading: Telling Yourself the Truth - William Backus & Marie Chapian

Ephesians 4:21-29

Since you have heard about Jesus and have learned the truth that comes from him, throw off your old sinful nature and your former way of life, which is corrupted by lust and deception. Instead, let the Spirit renew your thoughts and attitudes. Put on your new nature, created to be like God—truly righteous and holy. So stop telling lies. Let us tell our neighbors the truth, for we are all parts of the same body. And don't sin by letting anger control you. Don't let the sun go down while you are still angry, for anger gives a foothold to the devil. If you are a thief, quit stealing. Instead, use your hands for good hard work, and then give generously to others in need. Don't use foul or abusive language. Let everything you say be good and helpful, so that your words will be an encouragement to those who hear them.

Note:
The Bible tells us we cannot overcome our nature on our own strength. We need God's Spirit to give us a new nature, which will enable us to do the right thing and resist temptation.

Day Twenty-six: Whiter than White

Perhaps we can understand ourselves in relation to God with a visual metaphor. Imagine two large white spaces, each identical to the other, each the most beautiful, radiant white ever seen. This perfect whiteness resembles the purity, goodness, and righteousness of God. Now imagine the color of our character in relation to God. Would it be fair to picture each of us as tiny, gray dots, in between God's white and evil's black?

What if the gray of our imperfection is introduced to one of those pictures? Does it remain 100 percent pure white, without any blemish? Obviously not. The purity of the picture will be lost. But the other picture, untainted by our imperfection remains the same, because God's purity cannot be compromised. His perfection in love, goodness, passion, judgment, joy and peace will forever remain unchanged. Do we see the problem facing us? On one hand, we belong to God. He loves us and wants to hold us close and welcomes us into His presence. In fact, a relationship with Him is the reason for our existence!

On the other hand, perfection and imperfection are each others' opposites. We are the ones creating the distance. How do we expect a perfect God to condone imperfection? Is there hope for us to be reunited with God? Will divine intervention be able to undo our imperfection? If so, where do we go to seek help? Who can set us straight with God?

Hosea 3:5

In the last days, they will tremble in awe of the Lord and of his goodness.

Note:
If we need God's perfection in order to be welcomed by God, perhaps we should search for His perfection, rather than our own.

Day Twenty-seven: Serious Separation

We are created to be in an intimate, personal love relationship with God. It is the sole purpose for our being, yet the gap between God's character and ours is so enormous that, for most of us, no relationship exists at all.

This separation from God is the most serious issue we face. A world separated from God lacks the love we so desperately need. We seek happiness but look for it in the wrong places. Most of us settle for short-term counterfeits that need continual replenishing. We have given up on the deep joy and satisfaction for which we were created. We do not know what this joy or satisfaction is, nor do we know where to find it.

Do we really expect to know answers to life's questions apart from God? Would it not be more reasonable to ask our Creator, the Source of Life, for the secret to eternal happiness? If God created the universe and all life in it, shouldn't we go to Him for this knowledge?

God does hold the key to eternal love, joy and peace. In fact, He has done everything possible to let us know about this key. We need only to go to Him and listen to His gentle voice.

* Suggested further reading: Brokenness - Nancy Leigh DeMoss

Galatians 5:19-23

When you follow the desires of your sinful nature, the results are very clear: sexual immorality, impurity, lustful pleasures, idolatry, sorcery, hostility, quarreling, jealousy, outbursts of anger, selfish ambition, dissension, division, envy, drunkenness, wild parties, and other sins like these. Let me tell you again, as I have before, that anyone living that sort of life will not inherit the Kingdom of God. But the Holy Spirit produces this kind of fruit in our lives: love, joy, peace, patience, kindness, goodness, faithfulness, gentleness, and self-control. There is no law against these things!

Note:
Who wouldn't want to be inhabited by the Holy Spirit? We are so far separated from God, the Holy Spirit isn't even on our radar screen. If the Bible claims such love, joy and peace, shouldn't we check it out instead of ignoring it altogether?

Good News

Day Twenty-eight: Son of God

To love a spiritual God not seen, heard or touched is difficult. In His wisdom, God made Himself physical in the person of Jesus Christ. Jesus Christ is the bridge between God and mankind in many ways.

First, He came to roprocont Cod the Father, to show His people the love He has for us. He lovingly chose to exchange His limitlessness for the constraints of a human body.

Second, He came to share our struggle as humans, to fully experience our pain and sorrow. He came to show us the way to experience the intense love, joy and peace of living in harmony with God the Father.

Third, He came to fulfill the Law. Jesus is the only perfect human being ever to walk the earth. As intended by God, He is perfect love in action.

Fourth, He came to invite us to experience eternal life with Him and His Father in Heaven. The open invitation is always there, but He came to deliver it in person, representing Himself and His Father.

Fifth, He came to restore our relationship with God. Through Him, we are able to embrace God's love for us and once again be intimate with God for ever and ever. He is the solution to our problem.

Sixth, He came to pay the price of our wrongdoings. His shed blood washes away our every sin.

* Suggested further reading: The Passion of Jesus Christ - John Piper

Psalms 23

The Lord is my shepherd; I have all that I need.
He lets me rest in green meadows; he leads me beside
peaceful streams. He renews my strength.
He guides me along right paths, bringing honor to his name.
Even when I walk through the darkest valley,
I will not be afraid, for you are close beside me.
Your rod and your staff protect and comfort me.
You prepare a feast for me in the presence of my enemies.
You honor me by anointing my head with oil.
My cup overflows with blessings. Surely your goodness and
unfailing love will pursue me all the days of my life, and I will
live in the house of the Lord forever.

Note:
This is God's answer to man's struggle. The Father God we
have been missing, made known to us through His Son Jesus
Christ, our Lord and Savior.

Day Twenty-nine: Legend, Lunatic, Liar or Lord

Legends do not exist, lunatics are crazy, liars lie, and lords reign. Who is Jesus Christ?

Hardly anybody doubts Christ's existence. It would be quite outrageous to question it. Even those who do not believe He is the Son of God accept that He walked the earth. He is no legend.

Most religions accept Christ's status as a wise rabbi or teacher. His extraordinary statements, His unusual ability to interpret the Torah and His follower's statements qualify Him as perhaps the wisest person who ever lived. He is no lunatic.

If He lied about being the Son of God, knowing full well He was not, He would have been a messenger from Hell. Preaching a message of love and dying at the cross for a lie cannot be reconciled. His life was all about Truth. It is a Truth that will set you free. He is no liar.

Jesus Christ is Lord. His life, miracles, message, invitation, death, resurrection and ascension into Heaven all point toward His Heavenly Father. Jesus is the Son of God, God's answer to mankind's misery. He is our Lord and Savior.

* Suggested further reading: Mere Christianity - CS Lewis

1 Chronicles 29:10-13

O Lord, the God of our ancestor Israel, may you be praised forever and ever! Yours, O Lord, is the greatness, the power, the glory, the victory, and the majesty. Everything in the heavens and on earth is yours, O Lord, and this is your kingdom. We adore you as the one who is over all things. Wealth and honor come from you alone, for you rule over everything. Power and might are in your hand, and at your discretion people are made great and given strength. O our God, we thank you and praise your glorious name!

Note:
Jesus Christ influenced the world more than anybody. He never wrote a single piece of text. His ministry lasted only about three years. He traveled just a small area and had only 12 close disciples. We would be wise to find out His true origin.

Day Thirty: Light in Darkness

Created in the image of God, we recognize good from evil. Why then do we live in a dark, evil world? What's God's role in all of this?

Darkness can be defined as the "absence of light." Light is the presence of waves and particles, and darkness lacks waves and particles. Darkness is not a substance in itself, but the result of a substance missing.

Evil must be understood similarly. Love is substance and evil is the result of lacking that substance. Heaven is a place full of love. Hell is a place without love. Evil, therefore, is not something that can be created. Evil emerges as love diminishes.

God is the author of love, joy and peace. In fact, God is love. Evil is contradictory to God's nature. The essence of evil is absence of God. The closer we are to God, the further we distance ourselves from evil.

The first Adam sinned against God, and evil emerged. The second Adam, Jesus Christ, arrives as the Son of God and conquers evil. He is a light shining into the darkness.

* Suggested further reading: Grace Walk - Steve McVey

2 Corinthians 4:2-7

We tell the truth before God, and all who are honest know this. If the Good News we preach is hidden behind a veil, it is hidden only from people who are perishing. Satan, who is the god of this world, has blinded the minds of those who don't believe. They are unable to see the glorious light of the Good News. They don't understand this message about the glory of Christ, who is the exact likeness of God. You see, we don't go around preaching about ourselves. We preach that Jesus Christ is Lord, and we ourselves are your servants for Jesus' sake. For God, who said, "Let there be light in the darkness", has made this light shine in our hearts so we could know the glory of God that is seen in the face of Jesus Christ. We now have this light shining in our hearts, but we ourselves are like fragile clay jars containing this great treasure. This makes it clear that our great power is from God, not from ourselves.

Note:
Have you ever seen the bumper sticker, "Jesus is the answer?" It's true. Whatever we're looking for, we'll find in Him.

Day Thirty-one: Christ Crucified

An often misunderstood and debated subject is the crucifixion of Christ. His death on the cross was such an excruciating experience, most of us would prefer not to ponder it. Why did God participate in such a horrible, evil, loveless practice?

Christ's mission on earth came to fulfillment on the cross. The crucifixion was the largest anti-climax to a precious life, but in fact, it is the single most important event in history. The eternal destination of every human being hangs on that cross. At the cross our lives are freed and our relationship with God restored. The resurrection validates the transaction and secures it for eternity.

The horrible death Jesus Christ endured for our sake is the most loving act God could ever do to save His creation. By choosing death on the cross, God shows us His willingness to pay the ultimate price. By sacrificing His only Son, Father God regained relationship with His wayward people. Through Jesus' death, when the weight of all sin was laid upon Him, he shared in all the pain and suffering of the world.

We could not pay the price to settle our debt with God, so Christ paid the debt for us in full. He suffered, died and rose again to set free everyone who would accept His sacrifice on their behalf. We are free, indeed, by the blood of Christ.

* Suggested further reading: Love Walked Among Us - Paul E. Miller

Matthew 20:17-19

As Jesus was going up to Jerusalem, he took the twelve disciples aside privately and told them what was going to happen to him. "Listen", he said, "we're going up to Jerusalem, where the Son of Man will be betrayed to the leading priests and the teachers of religious law. They will sentence him to die. Then they will hand him over to the Romans to be mocked, flogged with a whip, and crucified. But on the third day he will be raised from the dead."

Note:
The crucifixion of Christ is perhaps the most difficult for us to understand. But it is central to God's plan to bring us back to Him. It is Jesus Who suffered out of love for His Father and for us all.

Day Thirty-two: Gospel

Gospel means good news. What an understatement! Is there a better term for describing the call to receive eternal life by the presence of the one and only loving God? In simple terms, the gospel describes what God put in motion in the beginning of time. It's a map, a way back to Him. He restores lost relationships for all eternity.

As we have seen, none of us is capable of fulfilling the law. We all miss the mark and are therefore lost. We are lost because we are no longer in relationship with our Creator. Having a direct and personal relationship with God is essential for deep and eternal joy. Without God in our lives, we are doomed to spend eternity outside of His presence, lacking His love and goodness.

The Gospel says the price has been paid in full. And all we need to do is claim our right to participate in the rewards. By accepting Christ's death on the cross as payment for our sins, we are wiped clean by His blood. The train ticket to life and fellowship with God has been bought and paid for; and all we have to do is claim the ticket and jump on board. Going on that train ride with Christ will start an unimaginable journey of love, joy and peace! As I said earlier, 'Good news is an understatement!'

* Suggested further reading: Getting the Gospel Right - RC Sproul

Titus 3:4-7

"When God our Savior revealed his kindness and love, he saved us, not because of the righteous things we had done, but because of his mercy. He washed away our sins, giving us a new birth and new life through the Holy Spirit. He generously poured out the Spirit upon us through Jesus Christ our Savior. Because of his grace he declared us righteous and gave us confidence that we will inherit eternal life."

Note:
Nothing even comes close to the life-changing impact of the Gospel. We have enormous difficulty accepting its full measure into eternity. What shall we do to embrace it?

Day Thirty-three: God's Gift

When God created the universe and all life in it, He had a clear plan to enjoy personal relationships with every single one of us. To make the plan meaningful, He gave us free choice with all the consequences of evil entering the world. Then, because we could not overcome evil by ourselves, He assured our salvation by providing someone who could do so for us.

We cannot earn salvation by ourselves. Inevitably, we will fail to follow God's law. But we *can* choose to accept God's free gift. At no cost to us, God sent His Son, Jesus Christ, to fulfill the law and become the perfectly innocent, human sacrifice, taking our place and settling our debt with God.

When we accept Christ, God no longer sees our sins. He sees us clean and able to stand before Him. No matter how grave our sin, God's grace is far greater. No matter how distant we are, how long we have doubted Him, or how hopeless we feel, He welcomes us with open arms. At the enormous expense of His Son, Jesus Christ's shed blood we are reborn.

By accepting the Father's gift, we honor Christ; and are welcomed into Heaven and eternal fellowship with God.

* Suggested further reading: The Answer - Randy Pope

Romans 5:15-19

But there is a great difference between Adam's sin and God's gracious gift. For the sin of this one man, Adam, brought death to many. But even greater is God's wonderful grace and his gift of forgiveness to many through this other man, Jesus Christ. And the result of God's gracious gift is very different from the result of that one man's sin. For Adam's sin led to condemnation, but God's free gift leads to our being made right with God, even though we are guilty of many sins. For the sin of this one man, Adam, caused death to rule over many. But even greater is God's wonderful grace and his gift of righteousness, for all who receive it will live in triumph over sin and death through this one man, Jesus Christ. Yes, Adam's one sin brings condemnation for everyone, but Christ's one act of righteousness brings a right relationship with God and new life for everyone. Because one person disobeyed God, many became sinners. But because one other person obeyed God, many will be made righteous.

Note:
This gift is greater than life itself: Eternity in God's presence. We will take a lifetime to begin to grasp God's love for all of us. It is infinite.

Day Thirty-four: Hope

"Hope" is a strange word. Some consider it a measure to make us feel better, yet believe it is not based on anything real. They say it is a crutch for the mentally and emotionally weak.

Here's the truth: hope believes in a future reality. Hope comes from God, and is based on His promise to deliver us from evil, save us from our sins, and stand by us in trials and tribulations. He will comfort us when we need it most, love us unconditionally, and reserve a room for us in His heavenly mansion.

Life without hope is bad for the soul. Deep joy rests in the hope God gives us. Our circumstances may be hopeless. We may be desperate and see no way out. We may have given up and thrown in the towel. We may be at the end of our rope. No matter the circumstance, God is stronger, more loving, more caring and in charge. He is the master of the universe, and He cares for us personally. His love for us knows no boundaries. He will carry us through life's struggles and lead us to greener pastures.

With Christ as our Lord and Savior, hope is a reality not yet seen, able to wipe away sorrow and secure our way to Heaven.

* Suggested further reading: When God Weeps - Joni Eareckson Tada & Steven Estes

Titus 2:11-14

For the grace of God has been revealed, bringing salvation to all people. And we are instructed to turn from godless living and sinful pleasures. We should live in this evil world with wisdom, righteousness, and devotion to God, while we look forward with hope to that wonderful day when the glory of our great God and Savior, Jesus Christ, will be revealed. He gave his life to free us from every kind of sin, to cleanse us, and to make us his very own people, totally committed to doing good deeds.

Note:
Plain and simple: Jesus is the answer. When our hope rests in Him, there is no mountain too high to overcome. Instead we will share in His glory.

Day Thirty-five: Win-Win

Is it strange to secure your joy in God? If we are created by God to be in a love relationship with Him, should we not expect to achieve real life satisfaction in Him? Isn't it logical that if He is our salvation, our longing and fulfillment for love, joy and peace will rest solely in Him?

There is satisfaction in giving to the poor, being in love, and building meaningful relationships. But let us imagine building a love relationship with God. Wouldn't that far outweigh everything else? It does. The deepest joy we will ever experience is contact with our Heavenly Father. Having the Light of the World, the Savior of our soul, the Prince of Peace on our side is extraordinary. Nothing can pierce our heart nor steal His love when His protection is on duty.

Having God become real and personal is the highlight of our lives. Furthermore, we will experience more deeply the true beauty of life. The color of true love will penetrate all aspects of our lives. We will grow into new beings, reborn children of God.

This is a win-win deal if ever there was one. We enter into a love relationship with God and grow to see the world through His love-filled eyes.

* Suggested further reading: The Joyful Christian - CS Lewis

John 3:16-17

For God loved the world so much that he gave his one and only Son, so that everyone who believes in him will not perish but have eternal life. God sent his Son into the world not to judge the world, but to save the world through him.

Note:
We will never love God as much and deeply as He loves us. To experience the love of God is the ultimate life has to offer. It starts with Christ on the cross, paying the price for our sin.

Day Thirty-six: Freeing Truth

We are heavy laden, our path is narrow and night is upon us. Can anybody brighten the day, show us the way and ease our burden? Who can save the lost, forgive sins and lead us into eternity?

God Almighty: our Father in Heaven, God Most High, Everlasting Father, Ancient of Days, God of Peace, Father of Mercies, God of Glory, the great I AM THAT I AM.

The Lord Jesus Christ, Light of the World, Lamb of God, King of Kings, Lord of Lords, Bread of Life, Shepherd of Souls, Fountain of Living Waters, Prince of Peace, Rock of Salvation.

The Holy Ghost: Helper, Comforter, Spirit of Truth, Holy Spirit of Promise.

God provides mercy for the guilty, grace for the undeserving. He is our shield and refuge. He keeps us from falling and gives us strength and power. He crowns us with loving-kindness and tender mercies.

It is the Son of God, Jesus Christ, Who takes away the sin of the world. He is the Way, the Truth and the Life. He is with us always and His truth will set us free.

* Suggested further reading: The Jesus I Never Knew - Philip Yancey

Luke 1:76-79

"And you, my little son, will be called the prophet of the Most High, because you will prepare the way for the Lord. You will tell his people how to find salvation through forgiveness of their sins. Because of God's tender mercy, the morning light from heaven is about to break upon us, to give light to those who sit in darkness and in the shadow of death, and to guide us to the path of peace."

Note:
Should we continue to deny our darkness and carry our burden? Or shall we run to God, embrace Jesus into our hearts, and welcome the Holy Spirit to guide us into the light of God?

Day Thirty-seven: Loved by God

A blind person cannot fully appreciate the beauty of colors, nor can a deaf person, the beauty of sound. So it is with the love of God. It can only be experienced first-hand. It is impossible to share how wonderful it is to be loved by God, or how fulfilling life becomes, if you don't know Him yourself.

Being in relationship with God is like living in a different, more beautiful world. We see everything through the lens of God's love. Life's perspectives dramatically improve through the hope we have in God. Eyes can see and ears can hear, where before we were blind and deaf. The glass is no longer half empty. Instead, we have full lives because our eyes are set on a bright beacon.

It is not as if we suddenly have our act together and can solve all of life's riddles. Life can still be difficult, but with God on our side, we can remain strong and positive. Even if we mess up again, we know we are going to be fine because God forgives us again and again. God wants the very best for us and He will provide. With God beside us, who or what can be against us?

He is God Almighty, our Father in Heaven, our creator, the Alpha and Omega. He is God Almighty, Jesus Christ, who died for us and loves us unconditionally forever and ever.

* Suggested further reading: The God You Can Know - Dan De Haan

Ephesians 3:14-21

When I think of all this, I fall to my knees and pray to the Father, the Creator of everything in heaven and on earth. I pray that from his glorious, unlimited resources he will empower you with inner strength through his Spirit. Then Christ will make his home in your hearts as you trust in him. Your roots will grow down into God's love and keep you strong. And may you have the power to understand, as all God's people should, how wide, how long, how high, and how deep his love is. May you experience the love of Christ, though it is too great to understand fully. Then you will be made complete with all the fullness of life and power that comes from God. Now all glory to God, who is able, through his mighty power at work within us, to accomplish infinitely more than we might ask or think. Glory to him in the church and in Christ Jesus through all generations forever and ever! Amen.

Note:
If we only knew....

Day Thirty-eight: Power of Prayer

There is no need to dress up before God, no need to study protocol, ring bells, or wait our turn. We simply go straight to the throne room. The king is ready to hear our petition. Prayer with God is simple. For starters, there is no protocol or escort. Our audience with God is instant and direct and we come as we are.

Why then do we not pray? Do we not know God loves and cares for us dearly? He does listen to our concerns and requests and knows the desires of our hearts. He wants to guide us, teach us, comfort us, and He does everything to help us reach our God-given potential.

The question is, "Do we *really* believe, that what we believe about God is *really* real?" The power of prayer rests with God. Our job is to make our appeals. God's job is to answer. If we know God is real, that His power and love are real, we can trust He shall respond. Once we accept this in our mind, heart and soul, we want to be with Him and He will be with us. Prayer becomes a continuous dialogue with our Creator. We fellowship with Him twenty-four hours a day, seven days a week. That is the real power of prayer—to know that when we call upon Him, He picks up, listens carefully and guides us to love, joy and peace.

* Suggested further reading: The Prayer that God Answers - Michael Youssef

Psalms 65:5

You faithfully answer our prayers
with awesome deeds,
O God our savior.
You are the hope of everyone on earth,
even those who sail on distant seas.

Note:
Perhaps it is time for us to pray and ask God to reveal
Himself to us. Are we ready to go to the Father and let Him
in? Do we dare to open our hearts and give ourselves to
Christ?

Day Thirty-nine: Homecoming

What a deep joy it is to come home, especially after a long and far away trip. It's such a relief to be back to our own stuff and, of course, back in our own bed and favorite chair. Best of all are the family hugs and kisses of those welcoming us home. Perhaps, an overly excited pet dog jumps all over us, expressing the joy of being together again.

Will coming home to our Heavenly Father be anything like this? May it even be better? Reuniting with God is like being reunited with a parent, spouse, sibling or child. It's as if we once enjoyed their complete love, but we lost it for years until one day we reunite again and enjoy the biggest hug ever. Those emotions are powerful, bringing tears to our eyes and a desire to never let go of this love again. We long to be embraced by never-ending love.

None of us can fully imagine being loved by God, but we can safely assume that experiencing the love of God will be pure, unconditional and not of this world. God's love is gentle and intense, overwhelming and humbling, joyous and sensitive, harmonious and life-shaking, patient and glorious, brand new and filling what lacked in our lives.

Our home coming to God, our Heavenly Father will be personal and unique. All of us will recognize Him as the missing piece of the puzzle. Our search will finally be over.

Luke 15:20-24

So he returned home to his father. And while he was still a long way off, his father saw him coming. Filled with love and compassion, he ran to his son, embraced him, and kissed him. His son said to him, 'Father, I have sinned against both heaven and you, and I am no longer worthy of being called your son.' But his father said to the servants, 'Quick! Bring the finest robe in the house and put it on him. Get a ring for his finger and sandals for his feet. And kill the calf we have been fattening. We must celebrate with a feast, for this son of mine was dead and has now returned to life. He was lost, but now he is found.'

Note:
To refer to God as the missing piece of the puzzle is not exactly respectful. He is the God of the universe! But even God lays down His title and comes running to us when we finally recognize He is truly our Father.

Day Forty: God's Invitation

The world is a tough place: people in pain, sorrow, hardship. We experience broken relationships. We suffer from unfulfilled dreams and life-threatening diseases. We have moments of happiness and love, but we know life could and should be a whole lot better.

God knows our trouble; there are no secrets for Him. He peeks into our hearts and loves us deeply. He has answers. He wants to restore what was lost. He desires a passionate, personal and intimate relationship with us. He promises us love, joy, peace, patience, kindness, goodness, faithfulness, gentleness, and self-control.

He sends His Son to bring us home. Our lives are made whole. No need to cry. Our sins have been forgiven. Our debt has been paid in full. The cross is our new reality. Christ's blood has cleansed us. We are free now. Our Father awaits us in Heaven.

Jesus reaches out His hand towards us. His soft, loving eyes penetrate deep into our soul and He whispers: "Follow Me." Once we were lost, but now we're saved. Our encounter with God has become reality. We are back home where we belong, safe in the hands of God the Son, God the Father, and God the Spirit who enters and renews our soul forevermore.

Matthew 11:28-30

Then Jesus said, "Come to me, all of you who are weary and carry heavy burdens, and I will give you rest. Take my yoke upon you. Let me teach you, because I am humble and gentle at heart, and you will find rest for your souls. For my yoke is easy to bear, and the burden I give you is light."

Note:
"Dear Father God, will you come into my life? Will you make yourself known to me? Will you guide me? I long for my search to be over. Will you reveal the truth and set me free? Will you help me with my troubles? Will you bring me peace and joy? Will you forgive me? I long to come home. In Jesus name, Amen."

Afterword

Dear Reader,

Thank you so very much for taking this "40-Day Journey" with me. I shared from the depths of my heart in an attempt to summarize what my own life's experiences have taught me. I respect your individuality and the choices you will make. No matter what, just remember God loves you!

My journey led me through deep valleys and luckily, some beautiful mountain peaks as well. But everything fades compared to my encounter with God. I am not sure of the exact day that I finally gave my life to Christ. About 10 years ago, God started to change me from the inside out.

My life's pursuit of *"Daily Happiness at the Least Cost"* slowly developed toward *"Deep Joy at the Grace of God."* It is important for you to understand that my only motivation in publishing this devotional book has been to share the love I received from God. It was at His direction that I developed the courage and inspiration to write. I pray that by following His lead, you will likewise embrace the love He has demonstrated to us through the sacrificial death of His Son Jesus.

With love, Otto

Revelation 22:16-29

"I, Jesus, have sent my angel to give you this message for the churches. I am both the source of David and the heir to his throne. I am the bright morning star." The Spirit and the bride say, "Come." Let anyone who hears this say, "Come." Let anyone who is thirsty come. Let anyone who desires drink freely from the water of life. And I solemnly declare to everyone who hears the words of prophecy written in this book: If anyone adds anything to what is written here, God will add to that person the plagues described in this book. And if anyone removes any of the words from this book of prophecy, God will remove that person's share in the tree of life and in the holy city that are described in this book. He who is the faithful witness to all these things says, "Yes, I am coming soon!"

Amen! Come, Lord Jesus! May the grace of the Lord Jesus be with God's holy people.

Bible verses:

Day 1	Genesis 1:1-5		Day 21	Matthew 22:36-40
Day 2	Revelation 1:8		Day 22	Exodus 20:1-17
Day 3	Hebrews 4:12-13		Day 23	Job 25:2-6
Day 4	Isaiah 40:28-31		Day 24	Isaiah 48:17-18
Day 5	Deuteronomy 31:6		Day 25	Ephesians 4:21-29
Day 6	Genesis 1:26-28		Day 26	Hosea 3:5
Day 7	Matthew 6:9-13		Day 27	Galatians 5:19-23
Day 8	Colossians 1:15-16		Day 28	Psalms 23
Day 9	Proverbs 1:1-7		Day 29	1 Chronicles 29:10-13
Day 10	Psalms 77:13-14		Day 30	2 Corinthians 4:2-7
Day 11	Romans 1:25		Day 31	Matthew 20:17-19
Day 12	Psalms 111:1-4		Day 32	Titus 3:4-7
Day 13	Matthew 6:19-21		Day 33	Romans 5:15-19
Day 14	Isaiah 45:18-19		Day 34	Titus 2:11-14
Day 15	Job 28:23-28		Day 35	John 3:16-17
Day 16	Revelation 4:8		Day 36	Luke 1:76-79
Day 17	1 Corinthians 13: 4-7		Day 37	Ephesians 3:14-21
Day 18	Jeremiah 13:15-17		Day 38	Psalms 65:5
Day 19	Job 9:2-4		Day 39	Luke 15:20-24
Day 20	Romans 3:19-23		Day 40	Matthew 11:28-30
				Revelation 22:16-29

Suggested Reading

God Are You There? - William Lane Craig

Does the Idea of God make Sense? - Charles Taliaferro

Defending Your Faith - RC Sproul

The Case for a Creator - Lee Strobel

Fatal Flaws - Hank Hanegraaff

The Design Revolution - William A. Dembski

Unshakable Foundations - N. Geisler & P. Bocchino

Creation as Science - Hugh Ross

The Farce of Evolution - Hank Hanegraaff

The Universe Next Door - James W. Sire

The Character of God - RC Sproul

The Holiness of God - RC Sproul

What's So Amazing about Grace? - Philip Yancey

God as He Longs for You to See Him - Chip Ingram

True for You, but Not for Me - Paul Copan

Can Man Live Without God - Ravi Zacharias

Telling Yourself the Truth - William Backus & Marie Chapian

Brokenness - Nancy Leigh DeMoss

The Passion of Jesus Christ - John Piper

Mere Christianity - CS Lewis

Grace Walk - Steve McVey

Love Walked Among Us - Paul E. Miller

Getting the Gospel Right - RC Sproul

The Answer - Randy Pope

When God Weeps - Joni Eareckson Tada & Steven Estes

The Joyful Christian - CS Lewis

The Jesus I Never Knew - Philip Yancey

The God You Can Know - Dan De Haan

The Prayer that God Answers - Michael Youssef

About the author

Otto Schultinge is a faithful follower of Christ; He soaks in the grace and love of God. As he traveled the world, he delved into the questions of life and came to the conclusion that God is real.

Comparing many of the world religions, philosophies and cults, he concluded that all but one are 'man-made'. Christianity only, offers a coherent, all-encompassing worldview, with a creator God at its foundation. As a thinker and philosopher the more he discovered about truth, the more he was drawn to scripture. In 2000 he accepted Christ as Lord and Savior, and is now an adopted son of God. Deeply enjoying the intimacy of a love relationship with the Creator of the world.

Otto was born in The Hague, The Netherlands and now resides in Atlanta, Georgia.

Made in the USA
Charleston, SC
14 June 2012